As spoken in Berwick

the unique dialect.........

A dialect dictionary

Fred Kennington

As spoken in Berwick

Fred Kennington

ISBN 0 9526496 5 9

Published by F.L.Kennington, Northumbria House, 35, Corbar Road, Stockport, Cheshire, SK2 6EP.

Printed by Parchment (Oxford) Ltd., Printworks, Crescent Road, Cowley, Oxford OX4 2PB

CONTENTS

INTRODUCTION

Berwick upon Tweed speaks..........a unique language. Is it a unique way of speaking? If it is then why is that so?

Berwick is a Border town. It lies right on the boundary between England and Scotland and is the only such town in Britain. Yes, there are other 'border' towns such as Carlisle, Chester and Shrewsbury but none stands right on the border nor has any changed hands between the English and Scottish or English and Welsh in the same way that Berwick has.
It changed hands fourteen times and was, at one time, a Royal Burgh of Scotland and its chief port. Back in the past legal enactments related to England, Wales, Scotland, Ireland and Berwick upon Tweed – not Carlisle or Chester but Berwick.
So much for its history but what has that to do with speech. Because it stands right on the Border consider how people speak on either side of that Border. As you travel north you'll pass 'Geordieland', Newcastle. Continuing, you'll move into Northumberland where the speech is Anglo-Saxon Northumbrian, not the same as Newcastle. That 'Northumbrian' remains in different degrees right up to the bounds of Berwick.
Now, if you go south from Edinburgh, the Lowland Scots spoken there changes as you approach the last Scottish County. Berwickshire. Lowland Scots spoken in Duns or Eyemouth is very much broader than that of Edinburgh.
Now listen to someone speaking in Burnmouth, six miles north of Berwick then listen to that from Wooler, fifteen miles south. They have the same historical basis but they sound quite different. In between the two stands Berwick. It is on the 'dialect boundary' between the two. It is neither Lowland Scots nor Northumbrian – it is unique to a very small area! I doubt if any comparably sized areas in Britain have such a diversity of dialect as found around Berwick.

If you are a Berwicker and you go across Europe with an ear open you'll find just how closely your dialect accords with the

Germanic languages. There is a lot more on that subject later on. Local dialects are not viewed with disdain in Europe. Yes, you need to be understood in other parts of Britain but local speech is part of one's local heritage and ought not to be killed off and replaced by horrors like the verb 'to rubbish'!

Fred Kennington.
Stockport.

January 2006.

DIALECT DICTIONARY.

In this first part I have tried to list as many of the dialect words used in the area and specifically in Berwick town. But there are also farming terms, fishing terms from Seahouses and Holy Island and Romany words. The latter come from Yetholm finding their way into Berwick speech as the gypsies travelled across the area. Many of these words have been passed down orally and not written. The spellings are my way to equate them with their pronunciation without using an 'academic' phonetic alphabet. And, by the way, there were differences between that spoken in the Greenses, in Tweedmouth and in Spittal!
Archaic words appear in the list, e.g. 'scumfish'. It has nothing to do with fish. It appears in 16C Scots texts meaning 'to smoke out', referring to attacks on Border houses or Pele towers when bales of straw were lit to smoke the inhabitants out, or suffocate them. Nowadays, when violence is more subtle, 'scumfish', in Berwick's vocabulary, means to be very hot, or airless, and I use it regularly.

If you go to the end of the dialect words listed there is a section on <u>pronunciation</u>. I hope you will read it.

Abbreviations used are: -
LS: Lowland Scots; NBL: Northumbrian; OE: Old English
SE: Standard English

<u>A</u>

aad	old (NBL, not Berwick)
'Abyssinia	this was the name given to Highfields Estate when built in 1935, the time of the Italian invasion of Abyssinia, now Ethiopia.
afore	before
Ah	I (a short, sharp sound)
ahint	behind

Arab	a 'native' of the former fishing community from Berwick's 'Greenses'.
ashet	large serving dish (French- assiette)
aye	'yes', when spoken with a long vowel but 'always' when spoken with a clipped vowel.

<u>B</u>

(at th') back o'	expression of time e.g. 'at the back o'nine' is 9.5 am or pm.
bad	ill – 'she's taken bad' more common in NBL.
badly liked	disliked – of a person.
baffs	shoes
baigie	a swede turnip.
bait	as well as in the normal context of fishing, it is the meal carried to work in a 'bait bag'. (NBL but never in LS where it becomes 'piece')
bahree	good, smart – Romany, commonly used by Berwick children.
barley	in children's' games when one child wanted to stop temporarily, perhaps to tie lace. 'Ah'm barley!'
bawd	bad.
bayren	child, but pronounced in Berwick not quite as LS.
bedfast	confined to bed.
belong	to be a native of e.g. 'he belongs Berwick'.
ben	an LS term heard, but uncommon in Berwick, meaning 'next to'. 'ben the hoose' is the house next door.
besom(bizzum)	never a brush – either an unpleasant woman or a troublesome child.
(buzzum)	a brush, but more NBL usage.
biddable	obedient, used to describe well behaved children or dogs!
bide	dwell e.g. 'he bides in Berwick' – but may not 'belong' Berwick. The imperfect is 'bid'.

bield	a shelter. There was a house on the Etal Road in Tweedmouth named 'Meat and Bield'.
birrell	twirl round.
blether	talk – also LS but not necessarily the same meaning.
bletherskite	a talkative person.
body	a person e.g. 'she's a canny body'. It comes from OE 'bodig' – a person.
bogie	handcart or make-shift cart built by children.
breed	bread.
browtins up	upbringing.
bucket	dustbin.
buckie	a stone, usually one thrown e.g. 'a muckle buckie'.
buleek walloper	cattle drover.
bummler	bee.

C

calla	fresh, cold referring to the weather, also 'calla herrin'.
canny	nice, or pleasant person, but also prudent or thrifty.
ca' canny!	slow down! Take it easy!
canny on!	as above.
carlins	hard black peas eaten on Carlin Sunday in Lent. Lenten Sundays are: - Tid; Mid; Misere; Carlin; Palm; Pace Egg Day.
carmel	caramel.
caul	a dam on the river.
caw	turn a handle.
chow	chew.
'churrch'	in Berwick the 'r' is heavily rolled – not so in NBL.
chowk	choke.
claes	clothes.
claggy	sticky, muddy.
claip	teller of tales – slang 'a grass'.

clap	stroke a cat.
clart	mud, dirt.
clarty	muddy, dirty.
clecken	group, gathering or large family LS.
cleek	hook
clever	often used in the negative to mean unwell – 'he's no' clever'.
clocker	a sitting hen.
cloot	a cloth or rag.
coa-na	corner
coble	fishing boat. They can be rowing boats used by salmon fishers on the Tweed – another type is used by sea fishermen.
coorse	coarse
copper	coal-fired wash boiler in washhouse (Berwick). In NBL it is a set pot.
cowf	cough
cowld	cold - in Berwick speech only.
cowp	a fall or overturning or, to overturn.
cowp her creel	give birth. Not thought to be an LS meaning. It also means to go head over heels.
cracket	low, three-legged stool.
crack	friendly chat.
craw	crow
croon	crown
'croon o'th' causeway'	centre of the road. 'sh'thinks sh'walks oan th'croon o' th'causeway. She thinks she's better than anybody else! Only the important citizens were allowed to walk along the centre of the road where there was paving.
croose	'divvent craw sae croose'. 'don't count your chickens....!
cud/cuddint	could/could not.
cuddy	a) a horse b) a saw stool
cushat	woodpigeon

'Czechoslovakia'	as with 'Abyssinia', the name given to the Billendean Estate when built in 1938 during the German invasion of that country. Shortened to 'the Checks'.

D

daft	either a) foolish or b) of low intellect
dahsent	dare not
darr-say	daresay, usually an affirmative answer to an invitation (Berwick)
(the) day	today. The word 'today' is rarely used.
daunder	stroll e.g. 'ah'll hev a bit daunder roond the Walls'.
'dear knows'	'I have no idea...'
dee	in Berwick it means 'to do', not 'to die'.
deed	dead, as well as the legal 'deed'.
deef	deaf.
deek	look (Romany)
div/divvent	do/ do not. 'divvent' is more common in Berwick. Both are common in NBL.
divot	a piece of turf.
donnert	the opposite of clever i.e. academically poor, but see also 'glaikit'. There is a difference in meaning between them.
dizzint	does not.
docken	the plant, dock.
'doin' away'	an answer to 'how are you?'
dook	swim (c.f. Dutch verb duiken = to swim)
doy	die.
dooncummer	downpipe.
dover	the water in which salmon has been boiled.
dowter	daughter.
dreep	lit. 'a drip', but used of a person 'a right dreep'
Drifter	a small trawler, either steam or motor.
drookt	soaked through.
drooth	thirst.
(a) drop	a small amount of e.g. 'a nice drop o' soup'
dross	small coal or coal dust.

drummly	muddy, usually referring to a stream i.e. 'a drummly burn'.
duckit (doocot)	literally a dovecot but not used as such. It usually suggests a tiny, cramped house – 'it's a right duckit'.
'ducks wi'veils'	type of savoury meat
duffy	outside toilet, the term more common in NBL.
dunch/dunt	push/knock.
dyke-back	field edge close to a hedge – to be cleared by hand.

E

Eck/Elleek	Alexander.
efter	after.
empy	empty.

F

facey	forward, insolent.
fadge	milk scone made without lard and cut in four.
faggot	always used to denote an unpleasant woman, never brushwood. In degree 'an owld faggot' Is more derogatory than 'bizzum'.
fair	as well as standard uses, it is often used to qualify in the sense of the superlative e.g. 'fair grawnd'; 'fair done' = very good; exhausted.
feard	afraid.
feardy-cush	coward.
fell	often used as a threat to strike i.e. 'Ah'll fell you!'
fettle	mood e.g. 'in a bad fettle', or a greeting 'what fettle?' = how are you?
flamer	an annoying person.
flittin'	moving house but it had an important meaning in the past. The May Term (12th May) was the date on which hired farm workers changed jobs, assuming they were

	not retained by their farmer. Living in tied houses, all farm workers had to move on the same day – 'the Flittin'.
folk	people – but the word 'people' is rarely, if ever used in Berwick speech – always 'folk'.
foozy	soft, mushy – in relation to vegetables.
for to + verb	used much in NBL but not in Berwick e.g. 'for to go'; 'for to do'. Similar to German usage – 'um zu gehen'; um zu tun'.
foosty	mouldy.
freend	friend.

G

gadgie	man – a Romany word.
galluses	mens' braces – an LS word.
gaun	going or gone.
'geezapeece'	a derogatory form for a stupid person.
git wrong	get into trouble, or worse – 'ye'll git right wrong!'
gey	very, but not excessive. 'gey cowld' is less cold than 'right cowld'.
gie	give.
(take the) gie	be stubborn.
girrn	whine, grumble.
glaikit	stupid – but see also 'donnert'. There are shades of meaning between them.
glidders	scree slopes - NBL
gliff	a fright.
(the) Goody Patchy	the footpath between Tweedmouth and Spittal, parallel to, but above, Dock Road. Presumably it refers to 'gutta percha'.
gowk	fool – often used on 1st April, but also an apple core.
greet	weep – a 'greetin' Teeny' is a grumbling woman.
grumphy)	all terms for a pig. In fishing communities the word 'pig' was thought unlucky and not used.
guffy)	
grecian)	

gud	good.
gudyin	a good one
'Gull'	sometimes used in a derogatory sense for a Holy Islander.
gulley	usually a large knife 'a muckle gulley'.

H

haalse/haase	throat (German – 'hals' = throat)
haar	sea mist common on the east coast.
hacky	very dirty.
'had away!'	'go away!' or 'I don't believe you!' but not in an offensive sense.
hainch	haunch.
haiver	talk a lot of nonsense.
hard up	as well as short of cash, it refers to someone's state of health. 'He's gey hard up' means 'he's quite ill'.
haud/haad	hold.
'haud ya wheesht	'be quiet!'.
haund	hand
haunds turrn	work, but in a negative sense – he's never done a haunds turrn aw day'.
heap-lie-on	a jumble of items; untidy.
hear tell	have news (of a person)
heather-louper	hiker
'hen'	a friendly greeting to a female, similar to 'luv', 'duck', used in other parts of the country.
hen-toed	walking with toes turned in.
hev	have.
hevtae	have to.
hing	hang.
'hing oan!'	'wait a minute!'.
hirple	walk with a limp.
hoolet	owl.
hotchin'	infested.
howk	dig up (potatoes, etc.)
howld	hold.

'How-way!'	'come on!' – opposite of 'had away!'.
hoy	throw; in Berwick it also means 'high'.
hoy oot	discard. A 'hoy-oot' was a practice of throwing coins to children at a wedding.
hunda	hundred (Norwegian – hundre)
hunkers	'sitting oan ya hunkers' is squatting down. A term used by miners when squatting down at the coal face to eat their 'bait'. Widely used in Berwick given the history of coal mining locally.

I

intilowper	interloper i.e not born locally.
i-ron	note that the 'r' is sounded

J

jarp	strike in a particular way. Hard-boiled eggs were 'jarped' at Easter.
jeest/jist	just – both used in Berwick.
jing-bang (lot)	the whole lot.
jougle	shake – but also in Romany, and used in Berwick it means a dog, usually a mongrel.
jowel	literally 'jewel', a name for a native of Spittal.

K

keek-hole	peep hole (Dutch kijken = to look; also Norwegian – kikke)
keeker	black eye – 'a right keeker'.
keen	a chapped place.
ken	know (German 'kennen' = to know) but see also 'knaw'.
kibble	hit with a stick, lit. 'punish'. It is derived from 'kibbling the corn' i.e. beating out the grain with a stick.

keir	a Romany word for 'house'. In Berwick it was often used to describe a small or dirty house. 'It's a right keir'.
kist	chest, usually to hold clothes. The fisher girls took their belongings in 'kists' when they followed the herring fleet round the coast from Oban to Lowestoft.
kitchen	living room. More commonly used in country areas where they had a big room where all daily work was done.
back kitchen	scullery. In Berwick 'kitchen' was more likely to be the scullery.
knaw	know, much used in Berwick. 'Ah knaw fine!'
kneeve	fist.

L

(git) laid oot	get in trouble from your parents.
laldy	get into serious trouble – you'll git laldy!'
lathered	sweating
(get a) lickin'	get a thrashing.
lift	steal.
like	a 'filler' word as often found in German viz. 'doch'. 'an whaat time dae ye lowse, like?' (what time do you finish work?)
'like-as-no'	very probable.
links	sausage – 'a pound o' links'.
Loanin'	a lane. Traditionally there was Cemetery Loanin' in Tweedmouth, now 'Inglified' into Cemetery Lane. In NBL, Loaning is replaced by Lonnen, and there is still the Bell Lonnen in Ord.
long since	a long time ago.
loose	as a noun, a louse.
loose/lowse	as a verb, finish work – originally applied to horses.
loosin' time	finishing time
lowsin' time	do which one depends where you live.
'loose-catcher'	the school nurse.

lot	this word is sometimes omitted whereby, e.g. 'what a lot of people!' becomes 'what a folk!'
lowp	leap, jump, climb on horseback (Norwegian – lope = to run ; German = laufen)
lowpin' stone	old stone steps to climb on horseback.
loys	lies.
loyer	liar – not uncommonly heard in Berwick – 'he's a loyer'. (Nothing to do with the legal profession!)
lum	chimney.
'the lum's ahad!'	'the chimney is on fire!'.
lug	noun – ear; verb – to carry. 'Cloath lugs' is someone who isn't listening.

<u>M</u>

maizer	a surprising person – mainly NBL.
mah	my (a short, sharp sound) A long sound 'Mar' is 'mother'.
mamp/mamph	hit a person
manishie	woman – Romany, not in common use now.
maun	man – in Berwick, not in NBL
meat	mainly in the country areas it was used for food. Farm workers who 'lived in' on farms described them as 'good meat houses' or 'bad meat houses' depending on the quality and quantity of meals.
'mealy Jimmy'	oatmeal pudding.
mense	courtesy – 'he's neither sense na' mense'.
merried	married.
messages	the shopping – in Berwick you go 'for the messages'.
midden	rubbish tip, dustbin – but not the same as today's domestic dustbin which was called 'the bucket'. Used also to describe a dirty person – 'they look like a midden!'.
mind	remember (a person or event) – 'dae ye mind Jimmy?' is to remember Jimmy, not to look after him.

mitter	matter 'whaat's the mitter?'.
(the) moarin	tomorrow.
mooth	mouth (of a person or river)
mooty	threadbare – lit. moth-eaten.
muckle big	very common expression although the words by themselves are common.
Myoonissipple	municipal – Berwick's 'Myoonissipple' Buildings.

N

nae/naen	none
naib'dy	nobody.
nebsy	nosey.
netty	outside dry toilet – NBL. The word was not used in Berwick itself where it would have been 'a droy lavvy'.
nicker	snigger (a person); neigh (a horse).
(the) night	tonight.
nip	a small whisky was always 'a nip'.
nithered	shivering with cold (but not fear).
nooled	kept down (of a person).
(the) now	just now.
'now then!'	a greeting – 'how are you!
nut	not as well as nut.

O

Owld Year's Night' 31st Dec. (Dutch – Oudejaarsavond)
'ower the bridge' go from Berwick to Tweedmouth or v.v.

owld	old – less used in NBL where replaced by 'aad'.
oxter	armpit.
oylind	island, or Ireland. (Norwegian – øy)

P

padeek	frog, toad.
padeekstool	toadstool.

passeej	the tunnel-like entrance to a yard in Berwick.
peenge	complain constantly, whine.
pickle	a small amount, a pinch, but note it does not take a preposition e.g. 'a pickle salt'.
'the pickters'	'the pictures' – the cinema.
pilatic	drunk (paralytic) – Berwick.
pinkie	the little finger.
pirn	a reel or bobbin for cotton.
(the) Plantin'	the 'Plantation' – the wooded section along the Tweed at the end of the New Road in Berwick.
plash	a very heavy shower of rain.
plenty	sufficient – 'hev ye had plenty?'
plodge	paddle in river or sea.
pluffer	peashooter.
Poalis	Police.
poadla	fish – probably immature coalfish caught at Berwick Quayside or near the river mouth.
poke	sack, bag.
'poor sowl'	'poor soul' – common expression of sympathy
pootha/pooda	powder.
poreless	lit. 'powerless' – helpless with laughter.
poss stick)	clothes washing item
poss tub)	do
'Prince'	a sarcastic term heard in Spittal and applied to either sex e.g. 'she's a Prince'!.
puggled	in a stupor.

<u>R</u>

rare	excellent. A 'rare' book is a good read and not one almost unobtainable.
reek	relative to a chimney – to smoke. A 'lum' always 'reeks'. 'Lang may ya lum reek an' ya pot boil! is a greeting on 'Owld Year's Night!' (German – riechen = to smoke)
rickle	painfully thin – 'he's jist a rickle o'bones'.
rift	usually a good time; a good laugh. 'We had a right rift!'.

right	other than the normal uses it is heard very often in Berwick for ‘very’ e.g. ‘ye’ll git right wrong!’. Comparable with German ‘recht’.
rind	white frost.
roan pipe	downpipe.
roond	round
rootle	throaty noise made by a dying person.
running (tide)	incoming tide.

<u>S</u>

sackless	idle or stupid person.
sair	sad, grievous.
salmon dover	water in which salmon is boiled and left to stand to prevent the cooked fish from drying out. (‘dover’ is the Celtic word for water)
scaffie	scavenger.
Scramas’n	Berwick pronunciation of ‘Scremerston’.
(be) scumfished	lit. overcome with heat. (an archaic term, still much used in Berwick, meaning ‘to be suffocated with smoke’) It dates back to pre-1603 Border warfare when fires were lit by raiders to burn out the people sheltering in pele towers.
scunner/be scunnered	sickened, had too much.
scroggie	crab apple, collected and used to make jelly.
seek	sick, most often means ‘fed up’ rather than physically sick.
set pot	coal-fired wash boiler (NBL) see also ‘copper’
shall	this auxiliary verb was not used in Berwick – ‘will’ is, or was, normal.
shabby	often denotes state of health, not clothing i.e. unwell. Commonly used throughout NBL.
(the) Shammels	various paths between the upper part of Berwick and the riverside at the New Road. Also known as the ‘Shammel Braes’.
sherrin	cow dung.
shiel	salmon fishers’ house along the Tweed.
shootha	shoulder.

shud/shuddint	should/should not.
shuggie boat	swing boat in a fairground.
sic	such.
simmet	undervest.
skelp	smack.
slaister	work messily, throw water about.
slaisterer	untidy worker.
slater	wood louse.
slake	waste land by riverside, subject to floods.
slavver	slobber.
sneck	door latch.
snib	as above, but one which also locks.
'son'	form of address to male – generally friendly, but can be sarcastic.
spelk	splinter.
spoach about	nose about, search.
spuggie	sparrow.
stameek	stomach.
stawnd	stand.
stell	1. artificial mound of rocks for fishing. 2. circular area enclosed by a wall as shelter for sheep on an open hillside.
stookie	to stand helpless 'like a stookie'.
stoond	throb painfully.
stoor	cloud of dust.
stot	bounce.
stottin'	bouncing, also boiling hard e.g. 'the pan's stottin'.
stovies	lit. stove potatoes – dish made form potatoes, onions and sometimes left over meat or sausage. Traditionally eaten midweek, using up the remains of the Sunday joint.
(take the) strunts	take offence.
starvation	often applied to the weather – 'it's starvation'
starvin'	implies hunger, not cold – 'ah'm starvin' o' hungah.
swalley	swallow.
swither/ be swithering	be undecided.

T

tablet	a hard, very sweet fudge
tacket	hobnail – 'tackety boots'.
take bad	take ill.
'Tammy Shops'	a row of old houses in Tweedmouth.
tangle	seaweed.
tarble	terrible.
taytie	potato. Immediately over the Border this becomes 'tatties' or 'tawtays'.
tee	too.
telt	past tense of told – 'dae as y'r telt!'.
that	so – 'ah'm that tired'.
thole	tolerate.
thoan/thoan-da	that one; over there.
thrapple	throat.
thrawn	stubborn, determined.
t-ow	verb – pull; noun – rope. (Norwegian - 'taū')
troot	trout.
troy/troyed	try/tried.
trow	trough.
turnip hole	turnip shed.
'Twempie'	native of Tweedmouth.

U

untle	until
used with	used to.

W

wah	our, but see also 'weer'.
wahnt	want, suggesting a mental deficiency – 'he's wahnt'n'.
wait oan	wait for, not act as a waiter
wallop eye	a 'standing eye'.
warn	the number 'one' as spoken in Berwick.
waysome	wayward.
wayze	whose.

weel kent	well known.
weer	our, ours, see also ''wah'.
whae	who.
what for?	why? – much more used in Berwick than 'why'.
whaup	curlew.
'wheesht'	'be quiet!'
'whole witter'	heavy rain – 'it's comin' doon whole witter!'.
wilks	whelks.
'will so'/'will sut'	heard in children's' arguments countering 'will not'.
willietuck	fish caught at mouth of Tweed (see also 'podla')
witter	water.
wud/wuddint	would/would not.
wummin	also used as emphasis in conversation – 'ay, my wummin'. Also heard as 'my maun'.

Y

ya	your
yaird	yard.
yak	Romany word – eye.
yark	strike (a person)
yin	one, 'that yin' = that one; 'thon yin' = that one over there. 'Yin' is LS for the numeral 'one' but it is not used in that way in Berwick – see 'warn'.
yow	ewe.

So much for the speech you hear, or speak, in Berwick itself, but there is a great variety of words relating to farming and fishing, for example. Salmon fishermen on the Tweed had their own vocabulary; those from Seahouses had a totally different vocabulary – so different that I have not attempted to include it here. Seahouses words were given to me by the late Andrew Craig Rutter. Another influence came from Romany speech, centred on Yetholm. All of these reflect the character and activities of these places.

TWEED SALMON FISHING TERMS.

These are some of the words found to date but the list is not comprehensive:-

alevin	recently hatched salmon, still carrying its yolk sac.
bag net	an illegal net.
bar net	a net creating a barrier to prevent fish from going upstream and thus thwart the efforts of other fishermen.
batt	artificial mound in the Tweed, or just offshore, used for salmon fishing. The most familiar was the Crabwater, on Berwick Pier, not now in use.
cairn net	stones piled in the river to create a calm area where the fish take refuge, enabling them to be caught in the net beyond.
ford net	used at fords or shallow points to catch running fish.
grilse	young salmon returning to the spawning grounds for the first time after a year or so at sea.
hang net	a net on poles placed in the sea below the high water mark.
kelt	a salmon that has returned to sea after spawning.
parr	young salmon about a year old.
'p-ow!'	'pull!', a shout by fishermen to pull the net in.
smolt	an 18 month old salmon that has yet to go to sea for the first time.
stell	artificial mound of rocks where fishing boats can be anchored. (see also 'batt')
stell net	one towed by the boat into the river in a semi-circular form and fixed by an anchor in midstream, the other end being held on shore or on a batt. When fish are seen to strike the net the men on shore haul it in. This

	was the traditional way of netting at the Crabwater and on the river.
trammel net	net used in areas of rapidly moving current.
wear shot net	one towed by the boat into the river or river mouth in a curve, then immediately drawn to the shore. This was used where the current was very strong e.g. Huds Head Fishery, Spittal.

FARMING TERMS

Agriculture has a large specialised vocabulary. These would not be used extensively by Berwick people but would be heard in the town on market days. Their importance is that most are now archaic, as jobs have been lost to mechanisation, and they need to be recorded.
Not included are many of the terms relating to sheep and cattle e.g. gimmer, wether, etc., nor have I attempted to list names of birds, animals, etc.

bittle	round, one-handed cylindrical beater, used when rolling bacon.
boarding rope	rope with attached eye used by byre men to bind and transport loose straw.
bondager	casual female labourer, an unmarried aunt or sister, to be provided by a farm worker when given the tenancy of a farm cottage. In the past, they were female farm workers who presented themselves at Hirings to find work. There is a considerable history to this term.
bratition	partition to separate materials.
bratty	apron made from a hessian sack.
brick	a section of a turnip field.
brime	horse's collar.
casting	a) clearing snow by hand b) dismantling the straw covering of a haystack c) throwing sheaves of corn from stack to a threshing machine.

cleek	gaff for poaching fish by lamplight – using carbide lamps.
crawcrook	implement for making straw ropes.
dess	part of a haystack, cut down with a hay knife.
dyetor	hand-operated corn dressing machine.
fiddle	implement for sowing seed by hand.
g-bald	implement for cutting thistles.
gin-gan(g)	circular structure in which a walking horse provided motive power to turn farm machinery.
gird	a) a frame one walks within to hold buckets clear of the legs when carrying household water b) a child's hoop.
graip	garden fork.
guddling	catching trout by hand by groping under stones or along the banks of a stream.
gumping	as 'guddling'.
harrow trees	system of beams linking horse collars to chains to keep horses' feet clear.
hemmel	cattle court for winter shelter.
herrd	shepherd (strongly rolled 'r')
in-bye	land near farm where animals are brought in to winter.
kirn	a) butter churn b) harvest supper and dance.
kyles	small piles of hay then forked together to form a 'hay pike'.
limmers	cart shafts.
out-bye	opposite of 'in-bye' i.e. the land away from the farm used for summer grazing – often hill or moorland.

pack	ewes, usually 10, being part of the shepherd's wage, and owned by him, but fed at the farmer's expense.
'peasie storm'	the last snowstorm of the winter. It occurs usually when the peewits are nesting and they suffer accordingly.
(hay) pike	hay, cut and dried in hayfield, then led into stackyard on a special 'bogie' to make the stack.
pingling	difficult or tiring farm work.
pirn	a) cotton reel b) loop of cord on a stick which was wound round a horse's nose to instil obedience through pain.
ploo(man)	plough(man)
rake-the-dyke	ewe that trails its lambs out from hedges.
ribber	implement used to cover seed sown in a corn drill.
scuffling	weeding turnips.
skep	straw beehive.
stubby	type of rag mat.
stuckin	stake to hold a string net and make a temporary fence.
syke	open gutter,
tob	flat nail for horseshoes (trade mark 'Mustad')
trivage	partition between two stable stalls.
'tumbling tam'	horse-drawn hay sweep.
tumpshie	turnip.
tun	container for animal food, capacity 1 ton.
ugly	sunshade, part of a bondager's costume, usually blue.
whitlins	young trout found in hill streams.
yetlin	three-legged cooking pot also able to be hung over an open fire on a 'swey'.
yell	ale, beer.
yen	oven.
yett	gate.
yep	an impudent child (ape).

ROMANY SPEECH.

Romany speech is, or was, commonly found in parts of Northumberland.
Originally, gypsies were settled in Yetholm in 1695 by a Capt. Bennett whose life had been saved by one of them. Their language, which is understood to come from a Hindustani or Sanskrit base, has virtually died out although some words are still to be heard in Berwick. They have been included in the main index. Since Romany is a subject of considerable size, no attempt has been made to explain it here. There are experts better qualified than the author to do so.

Based at Yetholm, the gypsies could be classified in two groups depending on their trade – either 'horners' or 'muggers'. The 'horners' made their articles from horn, e.g. spoons, etc.; the 'muggers' made other items e.g. pots and pans. They carried their wares round the countryside, taking regular routes and having their own places for overnight stops, or for bases. Where these bases were tends to reflect the quantity of Romany speech incorporated into the local patois. In Berwick, they came to Spittal where they fashioned their horn objects in the 'Horners' Burn'. One finds considerable Romany presence throughout Northumberland and the Borders. The annual Fair at St.Boswells attracted many.
Anyone wishing to learn more about the Yetholm gypsies should seek out information from local libraries.

PRONUNCIATION

A major problem I had – and I'm a 'native' speaker – was to describe the sounds of the speech. A direct comparison with Standard English (posh English?) was that Standard English (SE) does not contain certain of the sounds. The phonetics used in dictionaries are not going to be clear to some readers. As an example, bull, full, pull are commonly spoken with a short, clipped vowel – bul, ful, pul.

Another factor is the speed of speech. Words are run together – as in Dutch and German compound words – making it unintelligible to the stranger; - 'that'llhevtideethenow' = that will have to do just now.
The pronunciation of surnames did vary at one time but that feature is disappearing. Take the local name TURNBULL. South of Berwick, the 'ur' was spoken with pursed lips; in Berwick, the 'r' was, and still is, heavily rolled. As well, older people pronounced it as Trumble or Trummel, and those forms appear in Parish Registers. Another example is WAUGH, more common in Northumberland. It is not 'Wor' as in Evelyn or Auberon Waugh, but is 'Worf'.
Other common examples are; - Crummie = CROMBIE; Lowff = LOUGH; Wud = WOOD; Rippith = RIDPEATH or REDPATH; Boath-eek = BORTHWICK; Ellitt = ELLIOTT; Jimmyson = JAMESON or JAMIESON; similarly with Robbyson and Ritchison; Mattison = MATTHEWSON, MATHESON or MATTISON; Atchison = AITCHISON or ATKINSON.

Looking at the details of pronunciation, there are certain basic features:-

1. vowels are always pure and never contain the diphthongs of 'BBC' English.
2. 'h' at the beginning of a word is never dropped.
3. The glottal stop is either non-existent or very uncommon.

It is the vowels which stand on their own and their use can seem perverse:-

4. short 'a' as in SE bad, lad is 'aw' i.e. bad = bawd; lad = lawd – but not always. It is a lesser feature in e.g. sad, glad which are nearer to SE.
5. SE 'ie' or 'igh' as in die, high, lie, pie are sounded as 'oi' e.g. doi, hoi, loy, poi. This is harsh to unaccustomed ears but compare it with Norwegian 'høy' (high), øye (eye) which sound almost identical.
6. SE short 'o' as in cod, pod, Dod (George), are sounded with a long 'o' as in SE 'ode'.

7. SE long ‘o’ as in old, cold, sold are sounded ‘ow’ as owld, cowld, sowld, but this is not universal as bold, gold are close to SE. Hold is sounded as ‘howld’ in Berwick town, but ‘haad’ further south. Told may be heard as ‘towld’ but also as ‘telt’ in Berwick. Cold, in Berwick, is ‘cowld’, but ‘caad’ in NBL. This ‘ow’ sound is peculiar to Berwick and, having crossed the Border, it becomes the Lowland Scots ‘aw’, i.e.’cauld’.

8. SE ‘ou’ as in ground, round, sound, found are sounded as ‘oo’, i.e. groond, roond, etc.

9. the pronoun ‘me’ is usually expressed as ‘us’, but pronounced ‘is’.

10. SE ‘ah’ as garden, yard appears often, but not always, as ‘gairden’, yaird’.

11. SE ‘am going’ will be ‘am gawn’ in Berwick, but ‘gaan’ or ‘gannin’ in NBL.

12. ‘do not’ or ‘don’t’ may be either ‘divvent’ or ‘dinna’ even finding ‘dinna gaan’. ‘Divvent’ and ‘dinna’ are interchangeable in Berwick. ‘Do’ is pronounced ‘dee’.

13. ‘cannot’ is ‘canna’ in NBL, but ‘canny’ in Berwick. Thus, in Berwick, ‘canny’ may be either ‘cannot’; ‘canny’, as nice person; or ‘canny’, as to take it easy or steady.

14. SE ‘who’, ‘whose’, are spoken as ‘way’, ‘waze’ in Berwick.

15. SE ‘our’ may be ‘wa’ or ‘weer’ in Berwick.

16. SE ‘one’ is spoken as ‘warn’, or less frequently, as ‘yin’.

17.SE ‘all’ is LS ‘aw’ in Berwick, but ‘aal’ in NBL. Similarly, salt sausage, sauce often appear as ‘saalt’, ‘saasidge’ and ‘saas’.

18. SE ‘shall’ is not usually used in Berwick – always ‘will’

19. SE ‘ow’ and ‘ou’ as in powder and shoulder may, but not universally, be spoken as ‘pooda’, ‘pootha’ or ‘shootha’.

20. some ‘ford’ place names have an unusual pronunciation in NBL. Examples like Oxford, near Ancroft and Warenford do not have stress on the first syllable like Oxford University. ‘Ox’ and ‘ford’ are stressed equally with a slight pause in between.

The foregoing sets out only some of the pronunciations one might hear at the time of writing, or which have been used within living memory. But there are so many matters of detail I cannot possibly include them.

THE 'BORING' PART?

Have you ever wondered why different dialects exist and where they come from? I've gone back and looked through history or, better, 'etymology', the study of speech.

We talk about DIALECT and ACCENT, yet not knowing what each one is.

DIALECT refers to variations from 'standard' English in either, or both, Grammar and Vocabulary.

ACCENT refers to differences in pronunciation.

Thus, DIALECT, will, almost certainly, be spoken with a 'local' ACCENT but ACCENT may not use DIALECT. Speech may use the grammar and vocabulary of 'standard' English but be spoken with an accent. Were you to go back to pre-war days, BBC had its own 'stilted' speech; anything local was unacceptable. The first to break that barrier was Wilfred Pickles whose strong Yorkshire accent retained the grammar and vocabulary used by the BBC.

Anyone, for example, of Scots or Welsh descent will find it very difficult to lose the distinctive sound of their native speech and to try to do so can sound incongruous to the listener. Older Berwickers will remember the 'take-off' of the lady who reportedly said, 'mei bag's a broon bawg!'

THE DEVELOPMENT OF DIALECT.

The development of the English language over many centuries can be broken into four distinct stages. From within these stages the movement to the dialects of today can be traced. It will be apparent that 'Standard English', accepted today as 'good English', itself came from a dialect, but let us consider how the dialects of Berwick and its area fit in.

STAGE 1 - CELTIC.

The original language would be a dialect of Celtic, that of Britons of pre-Roman and Roman times. After the Viking/Anglo-Saxon invasions from the mid 5th century, the Britons were pushed westward into Strathclyde and Wales where Celtic languages remain.
There seems to be little of their language retained in the local dialect(s), but their influence remains in some place names: - Rivers Glen, Till, Tweed and the settlements of Mindrum, Kyloe, Ord and Pressen.

STAGE 2 – OLD ENGLISH

The first question must be 'what is Old English? Is it English, Anglo-Saxon or Old Norse? Look first at Bede's Ecclesiastical History of the English Nation. It reports the invasion of Britain in AD 449 by tribes from north west Europe – the Angles, Saxons and Jutes who came from what we now know as Holland, Denmark and Germany. Bede's History, written c. AD 731 quotes 'from the Angles are descended the East Angles, the Midland Angles, Mercians, all the race of the Northumbrians, that is, of those nations that dwell on the north side of the River Humber…'
The invaders were first referred to as Saxons, and subsequently Angles, regardless of the race from which they came. Prior to AD 1000, the nation was called Angelcynn, then Engalond, and the language as Englisc. The term 'Anglo-Saxon' came into use only after the Renaissance and covered all aspects of the culture and not merely the language.
Christian missionaries, led by Augustine, brought literacy and a Latin vocabulary with them in AD 597. Not surprisingly, many of the words brought by them are religious terms with no effect on dialect.

Then there is Old Norse. The Viking (Danish) raids on Britain started in AD 787 and lasted until c. AD 1000, bringing with them the Scandinavian influence. In the first hundred

years of their raids the Danes controlled most of eastern England and only their defeat by Alfred in AD 878 prevented a total conquest. The treaty that followed the Battle of Edington (Wiltshire, not Chirnside!) settled the Danes in the so-called Danelaw – the area east of a line from Chester to London and south of a line from Carlisle to the Tees, i.e. not the present day Northumberland. But Norsemen, from Norway, had settled in Shetland, moving on to the Hebrides and much of Ireland by c. AD 850.
It was this second 'linguistic invasion' that brought elements of Old Norse into English in both vocabulary and grammar.

Since the Danelaw did not affect Northumberland then there is little Scandinavian influence on place names in the area. The only Borough example is Lucker, but the influence does exist in surnames with the suffix 'son'.
But their influence is felt today in the similarity between 'broad' Tyneside and Norwegian. During the 1939-45 War many Norwegian refugees came to the area and had not too much difficulty in understanding the locals on Tyneside. Compare Norwegian 'hyem', 'hus' with Tyneside 'hyem', 'hoose' and 'tyebble'. The large department store on the Quayside at Bergen is 'Cløverhus'. The Norwegian pronunciation is exactly as it would be in broad Tyneside.

Old English was originally written in the Runic alphabet whose source is unknown but believed to date back to the 3rd century. It was used right across northern Europe and has been preserved in c.1000 inscriptions and some manuscripts. The most important Runic inscription remaining in Britain is that on Ruthwell Cross, Dumfries, dating from the 8th century and representing the Northumbrian dialect of the time.
In the two centuries before AD 1000 there was close enough contact between the Danish and Angle settlers to facilitate borrowing words. Both had a Germanic basis. Some of the commonest words in today's English came into the language at that time.

But a more weel-kent invasion – that from Normandy in 1066 – brought about greater linguistic change and the next stage of language development.
Everybody thinks of the Normans as being French but – they came originally of Viking stock (Northmen) who settled in the area, adopting the French language.

STAGE 3 – MIDDLE ENGLISH

With the Norman invasion came a French influence into the language, a process which only 'crept in' over three hundred years. But in this time there were major social changes and the advent of printing – the latter having a major impact on the language – which I'll come to later.
Post 1066 came the Domesday Book whose preparation took years and never even reached Northumberland. The nearest we have is the Boldon Book. Norse was still spoken widely through the 11th century.
Five basic dialect areas evolved in England:-

1. Northern – spoken north of a line from the Humber to Lancaster and extending into the eastern Lowlands of Scotland.
2. East Midland.
3. West Midland.
4. Kentish.
5. Southern.

These divisions are broadly similar to those found in Old English but with name changes. Northumbrian was now called 'Northern'; West Saxon was 'Southern'; the former Mercian was split into East and West Midlands. The background to the divisions in Old English reflected the native speech of the invading settlers i.e. Angles, Jutes, Norsemen, etc. The effects of these old dialects remain in the language today, hardly noticed. The word 'fox', with an 'f' sound reflects its northern origin while vixen, with a 'v' sound, reflects its southern origin.

In the 150 years between 1066 and 1204 – the year that King John lost control of Normandy to France – French was the language of government, law, administration and the Church, with some Latin in the latter. Thus the intake of French words into English in that period relates largely to officialdom. Old English could not be replaced overnight as had Celtic because of the strength of literature and the oral tradition.
The latter part of the 14th century, culminating in the work of Chaucer, produces poetry and prose illustrating the development of Middle English. Early in the 15th century, pronunciation had begun to change by what is known as the 'Great Vowel Shift'. This changed the sound of long vowels and a striking example is that Early English 'noo' became 'now'.
This was a turning point in the development of English after which the vocabulary continued to be enlarged – and still does so today – while pronunciation and grammar became more stabilised. That did not mean that everybody spoke a standard English. Dialects remained, but there was a more standardised form of the language. Times had changed from the forty vowels and consonants of the Old English language.

Over time, the EAST MIDLANDS dialect became the dominant influence in producing today's Standard English. There were good reasons for this. Not only was it the largest dialect area, containing the largest population, but it was also the wealthiest with its great woollen trade. Furthermore, it contained the capital, London, and the seats of learning, Oxford and Cambridge. These three places were the main social and political centres to which those wishing access to 'power' were drawn.
Lying between the Northern and Southern dialect areas, it provided a bridge between those two dialects which were not always mutually understandable.
This is what was written by the translator, John of Trevisa, in 1387 – 'men of myddel Engelond, as hyt were parteners of the endes, vnderstondeth betre the side longages, Northeron and Southeron, than Northeron and Southeron vnderstondeth eyther other'. A translation into current English appears

thus – and the words are not mine: - 'all the speech of the Northumbrians, and especially at York, is so sharp, piercing and grinding, and unformed, that we Southerners can hardly understand it'.

No doubt there are those who may be inclined to the same view today!

The next major factor was the introduction of printing in England by William Caxton in 1476. This was a major technological change. Not only did it help to develop a standard form of spelling and punctuation but it gave more people the opportunity to write and to have a wider circulation of literature despite the general lack of literacy.

Caxton, a merchant by profession, faced problems:-

1. given the differences in dialects, which variety of English should he choose?
2. how should it be spelt and punctuated?
3. should he use foreign loan words or native English, etc.?

Were he to sell books, they had to be understandable throughout the country. There is one example in a book dated 1490. It describes how some English merchants sailed into the Thames en route to Holland. One wanted to buy provisions and asked a local woman for 'eggys'. She couldn't understand him so another asked for 'eyren' She got that one right. But if a simple word like 'eggs' could not be understood, then you can appreciate the problem Caxton faced.

Caxton chose to use the East Midlands dialect – being the speech of the 'power base' of London, etc. Some of the 'funny' spellings we have nowadays date back to the days of Caxton and Chaucer. Scribes wrote down what they heard. If you research family history you'll know the many variations in names as recorded in old Parish Registers. Why do we have words like 'know' and 'knee', where we drop the 'k'.

The German word for 'knee' is 'knie' and both the 'k' and the 'e' are sounded.
This was also the period of 'exploration' when words of Spanish, Portuguese, etc. came in. Words like 'canoe' and 'cocoa'. You can blame Shakespeare for more words and idioms.
As the 18th century dawned, there was pressure to 'fix' English which brought about Dr.Johnson and the age of the dictionary.

WHAT ABOUT SCOTLAND AND ITS SPEECH?

So far only English has been mentioned. But Berwick lies on the Border. It changed hands many times so there must have been Scottish influence on the speech – and Scotland was a foreign country until 1603 (or 1707, if you wish).
Scotland was not subject to '1066' thus French words were not imported then. The lack of Norman influence and its remoteness produced a Scots English different from that further south. The conflicts between 1300 and 1600 increased those differences.
But there were also close connections between Scotland and France so they had some influence in bringing at least a little French influence into Scots speech. 'Ashet' is a common word in Berwick, imported from Scotland, but not so in England. It is a serving dish, the name coming from French 'assiette', a plate.
The Union of the Crowns in 1603 and the imposition of the Authorised Version of the Bible in 1637 brought the Scottish ruling classes slowly towards the use of 'southern' English, albeit it with a Scots accent. That was not always appreciated and both Burns and Scott did much to keep Lowland Scots alive and, of course, there is renewed interest in it.

STAGE 4 – STANDARD ENGLISH

As I mentioned earlier, there was pressure to 'fix' English and erode non-standard use. Technological change – again – would bring this about. The Industrial Revolution; the spread of railways and, later, universal education were the forces of change.
In the past, only a tiny minority had been educated – the medium later was the use of grammar text books so 'standard' English came to the masses.
Because Berwick was a remote place, untouched by the excesses of the Industrial Revolution, dialect would survive longer there. There is also the 'Border identity' preserved through both dialect and accent.
Even as I write this, I ask myself, 'what am I? Am I English or Scottish? I'm neither, I'm a 'Berwicker'!
Thankfully – for me, anyway –the 'silly' affectation required by the BBC and others pre-war has gone for ever.

But what about today's dialects in the Borough? Are they seen as ignorant and uneducated? The fact remains that, centuries ago, the East Midlands dialect predominated for various good reasons. Had history evolved differently then Northumbrian might have been the dominant dialect.
What do the professional linguists think? This is what one of them, Dennis Freeborn, wrote in his 1986 book, 'Varieties of English':-
'Prestige dialects and accents do not arise because of their beauty or linguistic superiority but because those who originally speak them are influential and others copy them.'
Unfortunately those in the media, who consider themselves influential, have brought in unwelcome prepositions like 'rup' and 'ron', as in 'draw rup' and 'draw ron' – the so-called intrusive 'r'.

Travelling in Europe with an ear open, one realises just how much of the present – and former – Berwick speech accords with the Germanic languages. So it retains its unique qualities.

Why should they be discarded except in situations where they would create problems for the listeners? So – we have to adapt at such times and be bi-lingual!

Consider the close links between the Berwick dialect and Dutch with whom trade has existed for centuries. The two have pronunciations – but not spellings – closely linked to one another – some say they are both unintelligible!
Just look at these examples:-

Standard English	Berwick	Dutch
bounce	stot	stoten, stoot
fool	gowk	gek
ill	seek	ziek
New Year's Eve	OldYear's Night	Oudejaarsavond
people	folk	volk
trousers	breeks	broek
walk	loup	lopen, loop

Well – those are the views of a 'genuine' Berwicker – what do YOU think?